The Roman

Introduction: How much did the Romans change Britain? 2
I   The invasion of Britain 4
II   The Celts 6
III The Romans invade 8
IV   The Roman army 12
V   Rebellion! 16
VI   Life in the town 18
VII The Romans at work 22
VIII The countryside 24
IX   The Romans at home 26
X   Leisure 30
XI   Religion 34
XII Trade 38
XIII Romanisation 40
XIV The end of Roman Britain 42
XV   The Roman legacy 44
Index 48

Introduction

The Romans were a powerful people who came from a country we now call Italy. About 2,000 years ago they ruled a huge empire. For hundreds of years Britain was part of the Roman Empire. It is called Britain today because the Romans gave it the name 'Britannia'. This book will help you find out some of the things that happened after the Romans came to Britain. It will also help you answer this question:

How much did the Romans change Britain?

You can find out what life was like in those times by using clues from the remains of buildings and from artefacts. Artefacts are things made by people. They are often dug up from the ground by archaeologists. In this book you will use photographs and drawings of buildings and objects, and you will read writing by people who lived at the time. These things are called sources and they will help you find out about what life was like then.

This map shows the names of the Celtic tribes and where they lived.

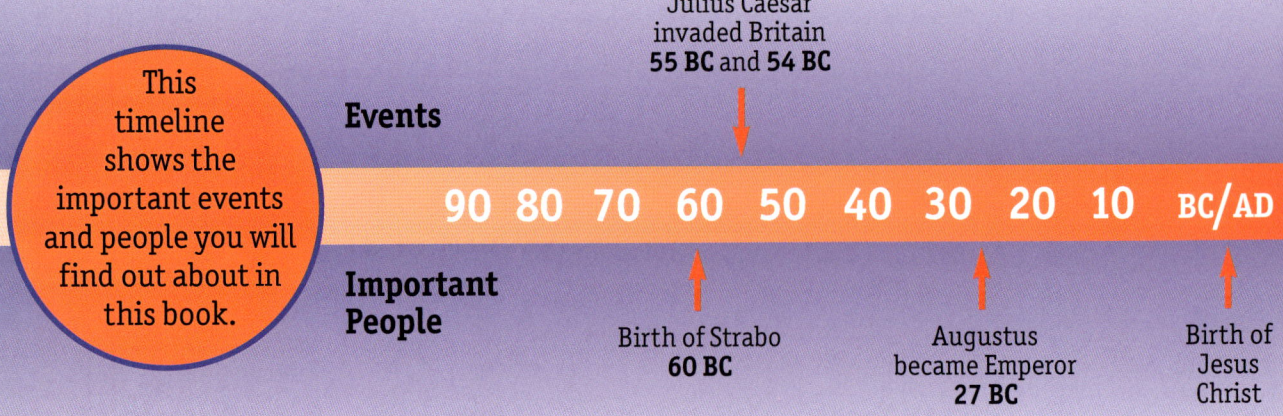

This timeline shows the important events and people you will find out about in this book.

Events

Julius Caesar invaded Britain
55 BC and **54 BC**

90 80 70 60 50 40 30 20 10 BC/AD

Important People

Birth of Strabo
60 BC

Augustus became Emperor
27 BC

Birth of Jesus Christ

The Celts

In this book you will also find out about the Celts – the people who lived in Britain when the Romans invaded. Celts had come to Britain from Europe to find good farming land. There were many different tribes living in Celtic Britain and they often fought against each other. Each tribe had a main settlement where it could meet and trade. Some of the tribes fought against the Romans but other Celts wanted the Romans to stay.

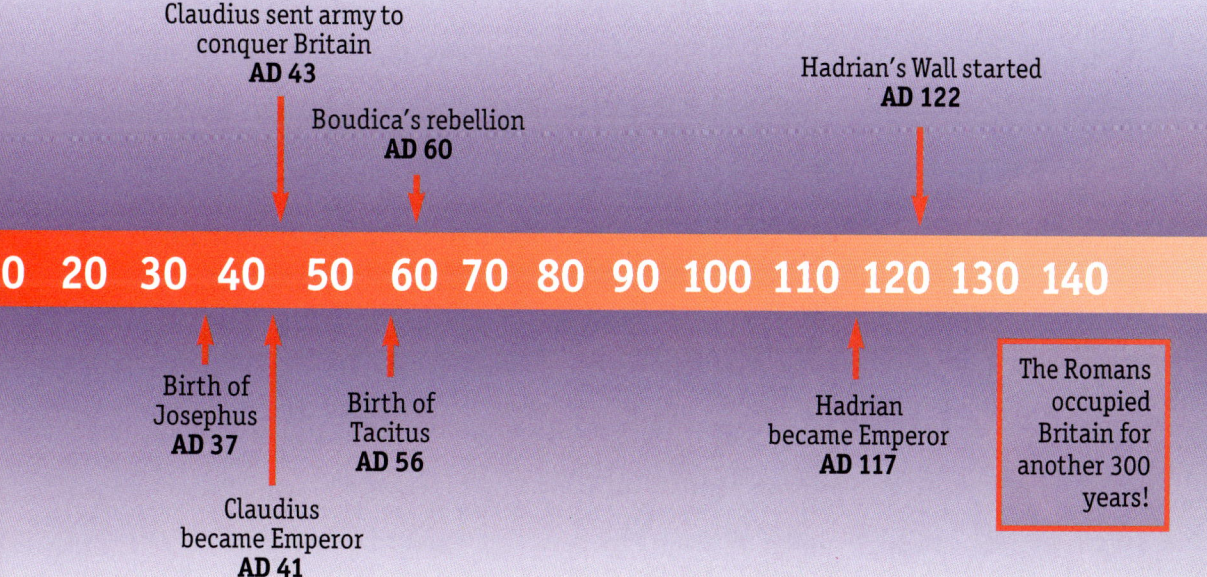

I The invasion of Britain

The Romans ruled over many lands. Their leaders wanted to make the Roman Empire as large as they could. Britain was on the edge of the Roman world but there were many reasons why the Roman leaders wanted to conquer it.

Why did the Romans invade?

Julius Caesar was the Roman leader in 55 BC. He had conquered Gaul, the country we now call France, and he wanted another victory. He came to Britain twice, firstly for a short time in 55 BC and then for two months the next year, in 54 BC, but he was forced to return to Gaul.

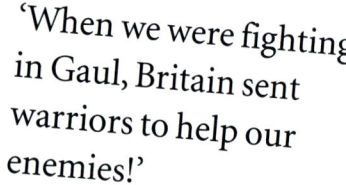

'When we were fighting in Gaul, Britain sent warriors to help our enemies!'

Julius Caesar

Things to do

- Read these two pages. Choose either Caesar or Claudius. Without mentioning his name write down what he was like and why he invaded Britain. Read your description to a friend. Can they guess who you have chosen?
- Why was Britain a good place for the Romans to invade?

Almost 100 years after the first Roman invasion of Britain, Claudius became the Roman emperor. He was not a great fighter, instead he liked to read and write books.

The emperor before Claudius had spent too much money. Claudius needed gold to pay the army and make the soldiers stay loyal to him. He had heard that there was gold and silver in Britain.

'Britain is the country I can conquer most easily. I need a victory to stay popular with everyone.'

Claudius

Then a Celtic leader, Verica, asked Claudius for help because his land had been taken away from him by other Celts. The map below shows the Roman Empire after the Romans invaded Britain in AD 43.

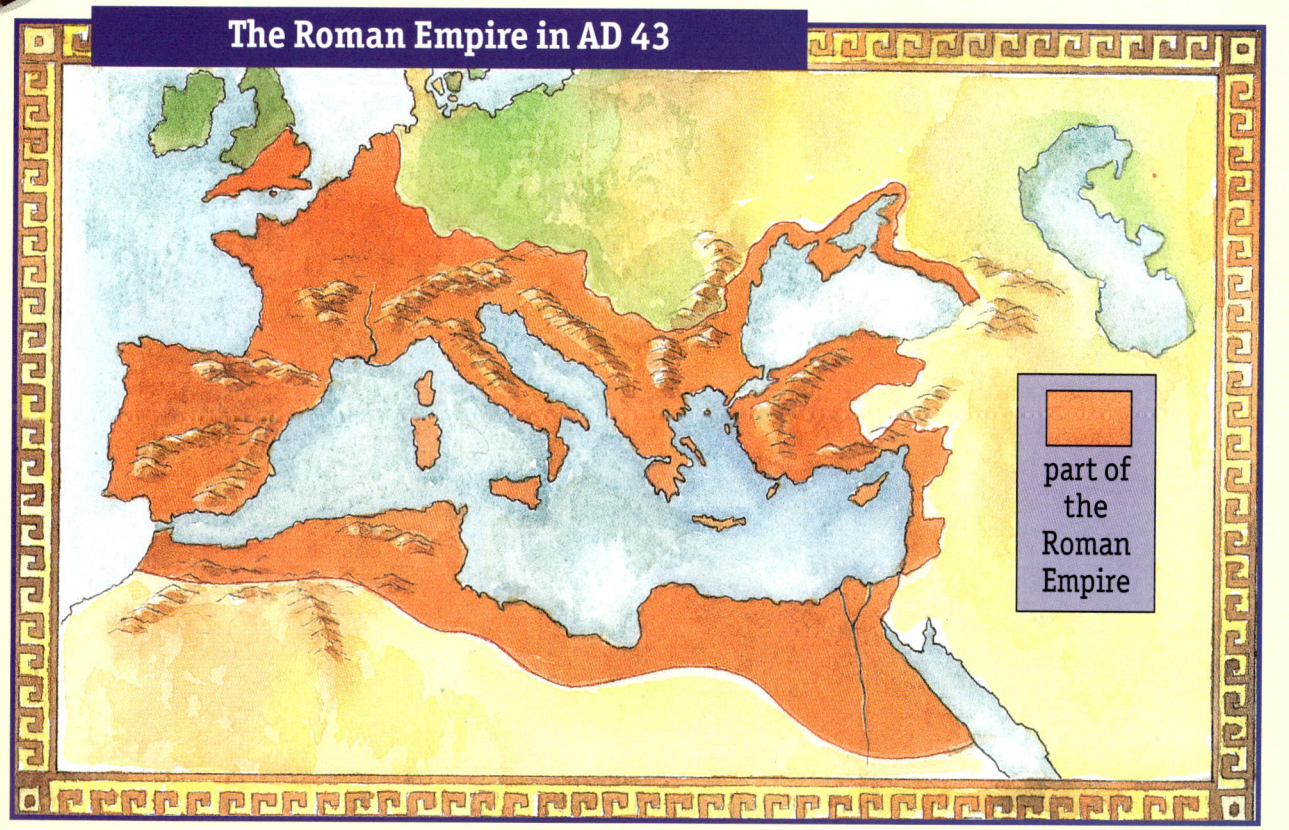

The Roman Empire in AD 43

part of the Roman Empire

5

II

The Celts

We know what Celtic Britain was like because people have found things from that time. We also have descriptions written by Romans but not by Celts because most of them could not write.

What was Celtic life like?

Britain was described by Strabo – a Roman citizen who lived about the time of Emperor Augustus.

Britain is triangular. It faces Gaul. Most of the island is level and wooded, but some parts are hilly. Britons buy jewellery and glass from Gaul. They sell corn, cattle, gold, silver and iron to other countries as well as leather, slaves and hunting dogs. There are several tribes. They make huts from felled trees where they live with their animals.

- How do you think Strabo might have found this out?

6

Some Celts lived in villages near water and good farming land. Some lived in hill-forts surrounded by ditches and high banks made of earth, timber and stone. You can still see the remains of Celtic hill-forts today.

The Celts wove cloth dyed in bright colours. They made beautiful jewellery from gold, silver or bronze. Weapons, tools and everyday artefacts were made of bone, flint, bronze and wood. Iron was becoming more important. It was strong and lasted a long time.

This is a modern picture of what life in a Celtic village was probably like.
- What skills did the Celts need to build their homes?

Think about
- Look at these two pages. Which parts of Celtic life has Strabo not described? Why?
- Why do you think the Celts often lived in hill-forts?
- What do you think were the problems of living in a hill-fort?

III The Romans invade

In AD 43, a fleet of Roman ships appeared off the south coast of Britain. A Roman general called Aulus Plautius and 40,000 soldiers were invading!

Why was the invasion successful?

The Roman army was made up of legions. Every legion had about 5,000 soldiers, called legionaries. Within each legion there were smaller groups called centuries. The officers in charge were called centurions. They sometimes treated the soldiers very harshly.

The Romans also used soldiers from countries they had conquered. They were called auxiliaries and had special fighting skills such as using a slingshot. Roman soldiers had to practise fighting, wrestling and swimming and do exercises. When the army was on the move they had to march for miles every day and build a camp every night. Some legionaries had special jobs such as being doctors, surveyors or blacksmiths.

Josephus, an historian writing in the 1st century, said:

Soldiers also carry a saw, basket, pick, axe, strap, bill-hook, chain and three days' rations.

- Why did the soldiers need these things as well as their weapons?

Think about

- Work with a partner. How many reasons can you think of to explain why the Roman army was so successful?

This is the tombstone of Marcus Favonius Facilis who was a centurion.
- What can you tell about centurions from the tombstone?

Two of the soldiers in this picture had special jobs. They wore symbols of their bravery.
- What jobs are these soldiers doing?
- What special symbols of bravery are they wearing?

The Celts fight back

The Celts were brave and very good at fighting, especially in their chariots. But most of them were farmers and could not spend too much time away from their farms. They were not well organised like the Roman army because all the tribes had different leaders and some fought against each other.

After the Romans landed they moved northwards, driving the Celts back. Some of the Celtic leaders surrendered but others carried on fighting. The Roman emperor Claudius was sent for. He brought some elephants with him! After Colchester was captured and 11 British kings surrendered, Claudius went back to Italy. When he arrived in Rome, Claudius renamed his son Britannicus.

Even then, not all the tribes had surrendered. Many Celts still defended their hill-forts. The Romans attacked them with powerful weapons like huge catapults which fired rocks and large, metal darts.

The Roman writer Vegetius said:

The Roman legion wins because of the number of soldiers and the types of war machines it uses.

Things to do

- Compare the Celtic warriors with the Roman legionaries. Which side do you think won?
- Find out what happened at Maiden Castle.
- How many reasons can you give to explain why the winners won the battle?

This modern picture shows the Romans attacking the Celtic hill-fort of Maiden Castle.

IV

The Roman army

The Roman army was made up of men from all over the Empire. When they came to Britain they needed somewhere to live, food, drink, things to do in their leisure time and places to worship their gods.

What changes did the Roman army bring?

Most Roman soldiers lived in forts. At first these were wooden but they were soon rebuilt in stone. Many of the forts that we can visit today were part of Hadrian's Wall which stretched 117 km right across northern Britain. Hadrian was a Roman emperor. In AD 122 he decided not to make the Empire any bigger but to build strong frontiers. There were forts and look-out turrets all along the wall. It had ditches to the north and south of it. Hadrian's Wall took the soldiers about four years to build.

This picture shows you part of what is left of Hadrian's Wall.

Villages grew up around many of the forts. Some soldiers married Celtic women, and this is where their families lived. Traders and craftsmen had shops there.

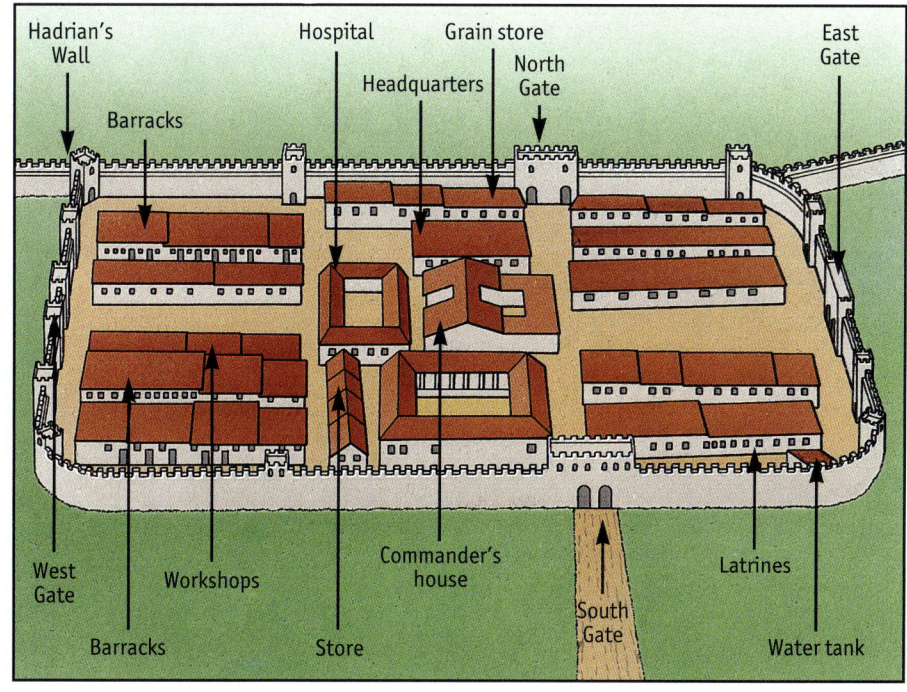

◀ This modern plan shows you what one fort on Hadrian's Wall looked like. It was called Housesteads.
- How is a Roman fort different from a hill-fort?

Soldiers were very religious. They worshipped Roman gods, the emperor and gods from other parts of the Empire. Mithras, a Persian sun-god, was popular. Only men could worship Mithras and their meetings were secret. Most Celts had never heard of these gods.

◀ This picture shows the ruins of the temple of Mithras at Carrawburgh near Hadrian's Wall.
- Find the entrance and the altar.

13

An army on the move

When the Romans invaded a country, the army had to be able to move with their supplies and equipment as quickly and as safely as possible. Britain had no proper roads so Roman soldiers soon started planning and building them. Sometimes Celtic slaves were forced to help.

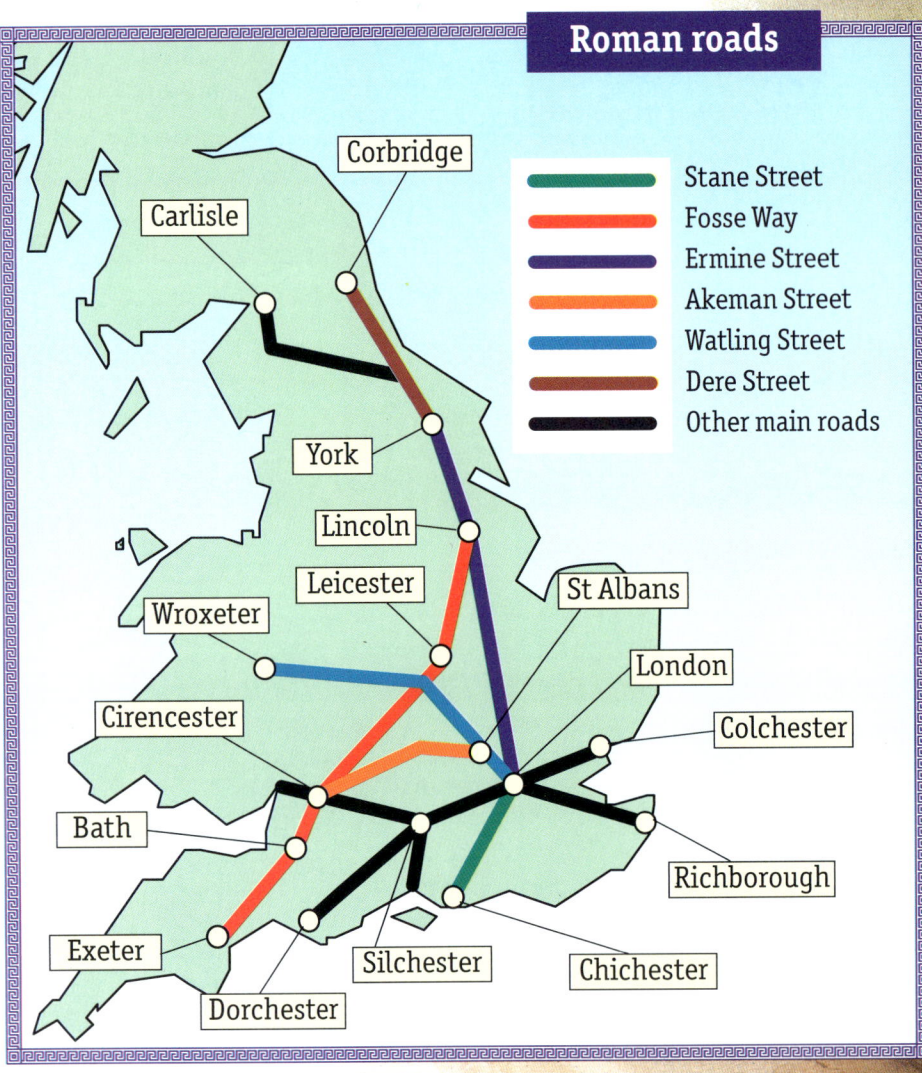

▲ This map shows the main roads in Roman Britain.
- Look at a modern road atlas of Britain. Which Roman routes are still used?
- Why were their roads as straight as possible?

▼ This is a modern picture of the Roman army building a road.
- The surveyor at the front of the picture is using a groma. What do you think it is used for?

▲ You can still see the remains of some Roman roads in Britain today.
- Why do you think they have lasted such a long time?

Things to do

- Imagine you are a Celt living in a village near a Roman fort. Make a list of all the things that changed because the Romans invaded.

- How many are good changes and how many are bad for you?

15

V Rebellion!

Some Celts disliked the way they were treated by the Romans and fought back against the soldiers. The most famous rebel was Boudica, the leader of the Iceni tribe.

Why did the Celts rebel?

Boudica's husband, King Prasutagus, died. He left half his land to his daughters and half to the Roman emperor. The Romans wanted it all. They beat the women, stole their property and treated the Iceni like slaves. Boudica took revenge. She gathered troops from several tribes. In AD 60 her army attacked and burned three Roman towns: Colchester, London and St Albans. The Celts killed thousands of people and destroyed the important Temple of Claudius. The Romans fought Boudica's army and killed nearly everyone including women and children. Boudica escaped but died soon afterwards. She probably took poison.

The Romans:

- introduced Roman laws and gods
- took land from the Celtic farmers
- encouraged the Celts to speak Latin (the Roman language) and wear Roman clothes
- killed all the Druids, the Celts' religious leaders
- stopped the tribes fighting each other
- made the Celts pay taxes.

- Look at this modern picture of Boudica. Which details do you think are based on sources? What things might the artist have had to guess about?

Who was Boudica?

▲ This picture was drawn much later than Roman times.

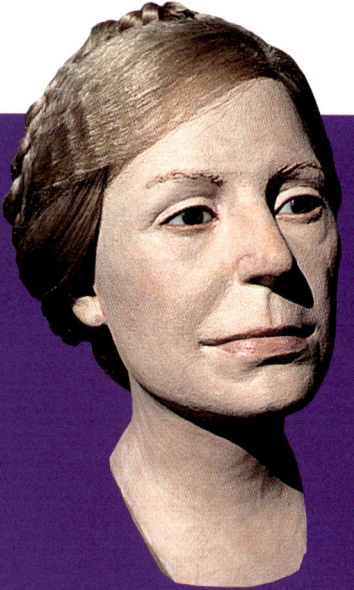

◀ This model was made in 1995. It is based on a skull found in Gloucestershire. Some people think it could be Boudica's skull.

This is how Boudica was described by a Roman writer:

> She was very tall and looked terrifying. Her eyes flashed and her voice was harsh. She had long red hair, and a torc (a solid gold necklace) around her neck. She wore a tartan dress and she held a spear.

- How fair do you think the Roman writer would have been in describing Boudica?

Things to do

- If you were a Celtic leader, how would you persuade your tribe to rebel? Give as many reasons as you can.
- Compare the images of Boudica with the Roman writer's description. How accurate are the pictures?
- Draw a picture of Boudica, using all the information you know about her and about Celtic life.

VI Life in the town

Many new towns were built in Britain during Roman times. Some were market towns, some were ports and some were at important crossing places on roads and rivers. Towns were built to house retired soldiers and small towns grew up near forts. One town was called Silchester. It was similar to other Roman towns in Britain.

What was it like to live in a Roman town like Silchester?

The Romans often built on Celtic sites. Silchester was a Roman town built on the site of the capital of the Atrebates tribe. The most important part of the town was right at the centre. A large building called the basilica faced an open area called the forum. The forum was used as a market and meeting place. The basilica was like a town hall and a law court. The other three sides of the forum were lined with rows of small shops.

This is a photograph taken from the air. Under these fields, archaeologists found the remains of Roman Silchester.

- What do you think the marks on the fields show?

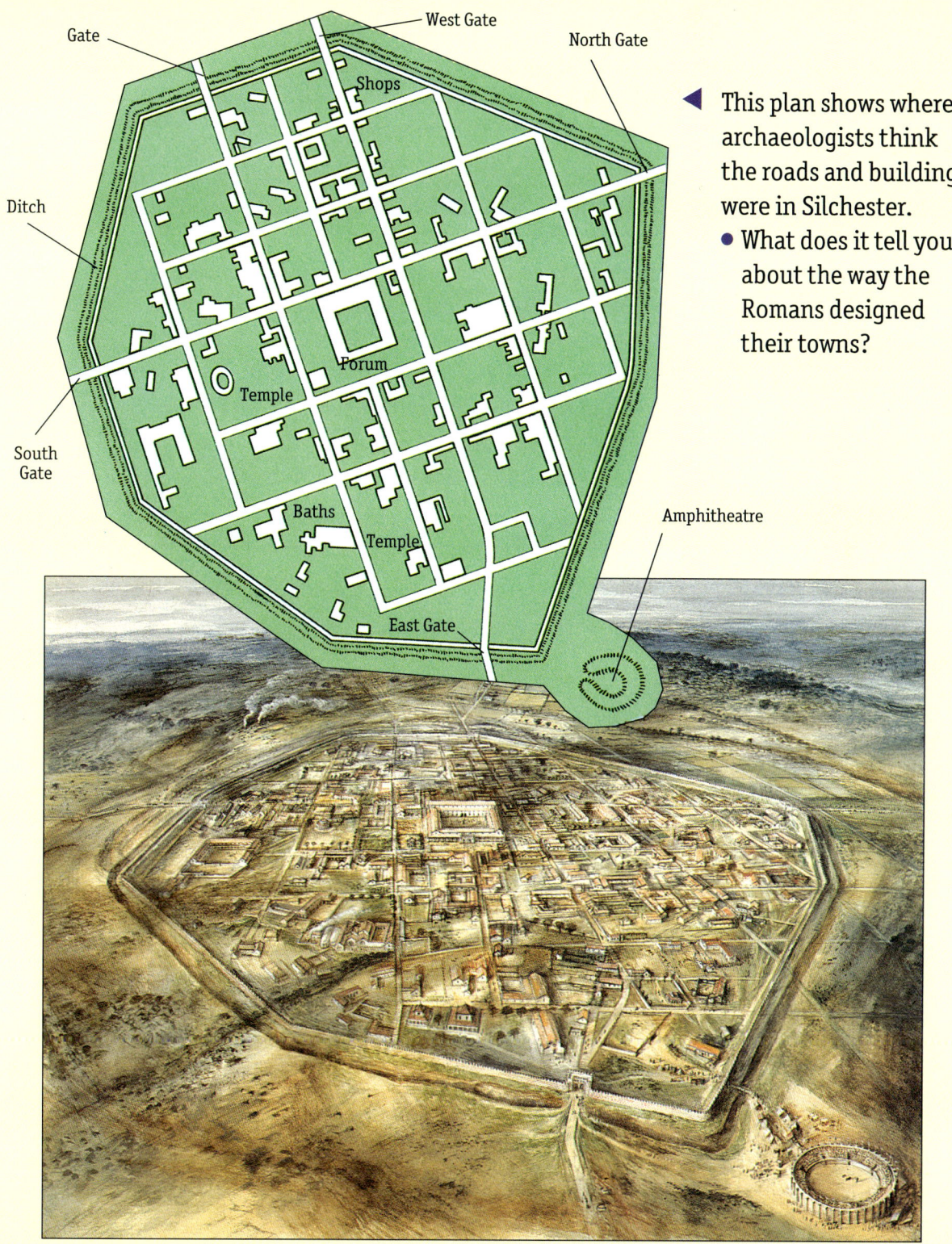

◀ This plan shows where archaeologists think the roads and buildings were in Silchester.
• What does it tell you about the way the Romans designed their towns?

▲ This is a picture of what an artist thought Silchester looked like in Roman times. It is based on what archaeologists have found.

• Match up the buildings and roads in the picture and the plan.

Town houses

In Silchester, archaeologists have found the remains of houses of different sizes. Some of the small houses were also shops. They were built facing the street with living rooms at the back. Rich people lived in much bigger houses. They were built around courtyards. Inside they had tiled or mosaic floors and painted walls.

The Romans told Celtic leaders to build houses in towns. They lent them money and builders to do this. These Celts began to live like Romans. Most Celts, however, carried on living as they had before.

This modern picture shows what a large courtyard house in Silchester may have looked like. It probably stood on a street corner and had a garden with flowers and herbs.

Some things the Romans did in their towns seem quite modern. Their towns had a water supply. The water flowed to and from the public baths and street fountains. Rich people had their houses connected to the water supply. Some of the houses had their own private bath houses and central heating. The central heating was called a hypocaust.

▲ The diagram shows how the central heating system worked.

◀ This photograph shows part of the remains of a Roman house. You can see the tile piles under the floor.
- Using the diagram and the picture to help you, explain how the houses were heated.

Things to do

- Why would Celts have moved to the new towns?
- Write a description of what it was like to live in Silchester using the information in this unit. Draw a picture of life in the town to go with your description. Make sure your drawing is accurate.

VII The Romans at work

We know that there were many people in Roman towns doing different jobs because of the artefacts that archaeologists have found.

What jobs did the Romans do?

These pictures show some artefacts found in Silchester.

- Are they like objects we use today? Have they changed since Roman times?

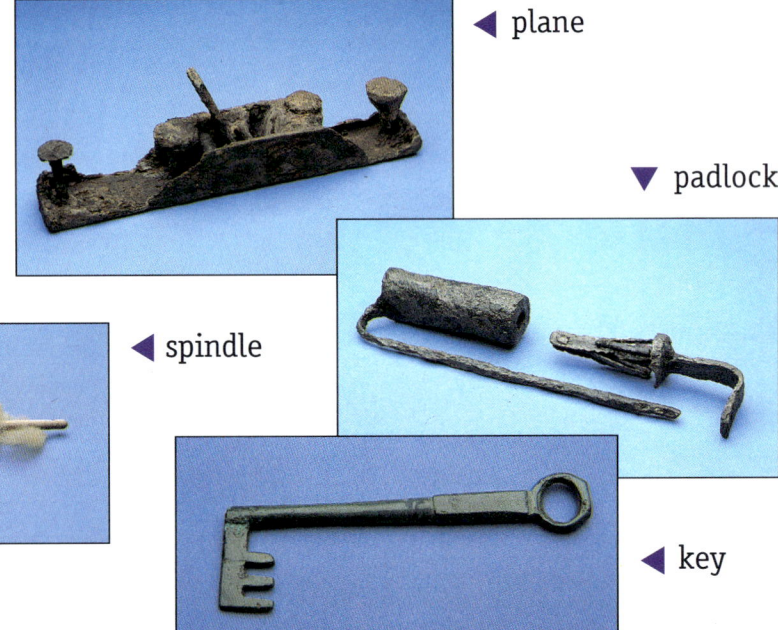

◀ plane

▼ padlock

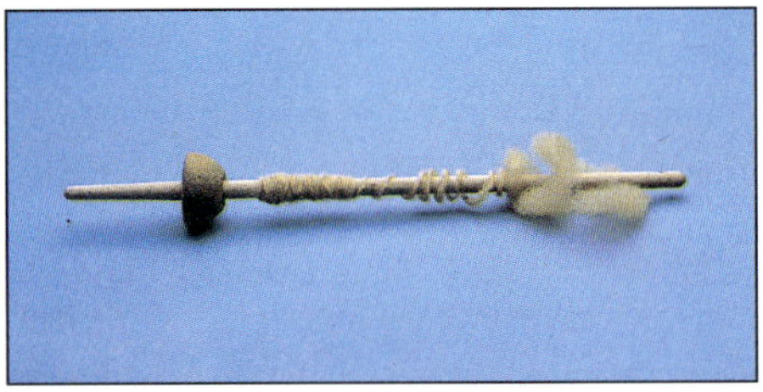

◀ spindle

◀ key

◀ roof tile

The tilemaker wrote the Latin word 'Satis' (enough) on it before the clay was dry.

- Why do you think he did this?

Think about

These objects were also found in Silchester.

   pots
   chisel
   needles and leather
   hammer

- How many jobs can you think of which are connected to these artefacts?

Roman jewellery

Some of the craftsmen in Silchester made special objects rather than everyday things. Roman people loved to wear jewellery. They fastened their cloaks and tunics with brooches.

Here are some pieces of jewellery from Silchester. The jewellers would use gold, silver, bronze, copper, jet and glass.

▲ This is a very small gold ring with a garnet stone. It was found in Silchester.
- Who do you think could have owned it?

Things to do

- Draw pictures of some Roman artefacts found in Silchester. Who made or used each artefact? Write the name of their job next to each picture.

- Which craftsmen would be needed to build a Roman house?

VIII The countryside

In Roman Britain most people – Romans and Celts – lived in the countryside. They grew crops of wheat, oats and barley, and raised cattle, sheep and pigs.

How did the Romans change the countryside?

The Romans needed a great deal of corn. They bought some of it, and took some from the Celts as tax. The Romans also brought to Britain some of their favourite foods like cabbages, carrots, pears and plums. People in Britain had not eaten these before. Ordinary Celts in Britain did not have a wide choice of food, although they did hunt animals for meat. Very poor people ate porridge.

This bronze statue was found in the north of Britain.
- What does it tell us about country life?
- Do you think think the ploughman was a Roman or a Celt?

Think about

- Which group of men were too busy to farm for themselves and needed grain, leather, wool and meat?
- What did the Celts need from the countryside?

24

Rich Celtic and Roman families lived country houses called 'villas'. Some villas were very large and had a hypocaust, baths and tiled roofs. They were usually built within a half day's journey of a town or main road. Most villas were surrounded by farm land on which slaves worked. Many other Britons still lived on small farms. These had not changed much since before the Roman invasion.

▶ This mosaic is called *Summer*. Mosaics are designs made from tiny pieces of marble, glass or tile.
- Design a mosaic for another season to show life in the countryside.

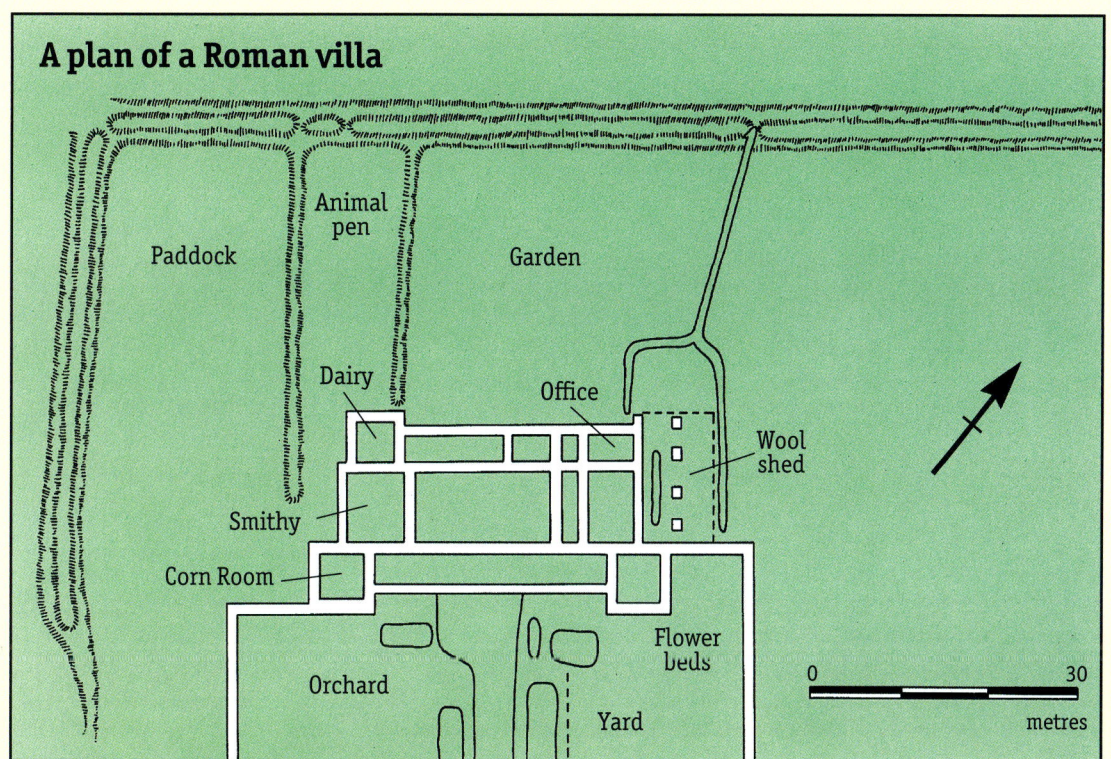

A plan of a Roman villa

▲ This is a plan of a Roman villa in Gloucestershire.
- What clues might archaeologists have found that told them what the buildings were used for?
- Imagine you are a rich Roman who wants to build a new villa. Make a list of all the things to think about as you choose the best place.

The Romans at home

Whether they were in the town or in the country, most Roman homes were very comfortable. The homes of rich Romans often had beautiful mosaic floors and painted walls but they were furnished quite simply.

What was life like in the home of a rich Roman?

Even rich Romans did not have as much furniture in their houses as we have today. Most of it was made of wood or wicker work. Expensive furniture was sometimes beautifully decorated.

▲ This room was made recently to show what a Roman dining room would look like.
  • Why do you think archaeologists do not find much Roman furniture?

The Romans brought different styles of clothing to Britain. A rich man would sometimes wear a toga. This was made from a long semi-circular piece of white cloth that wrapped round the body. Women wore long coloured dresses called stolas. In cold weather the Romans needed thick cloaks. On their feet they wore sandals or shoes.

Roman women liked wearing make up and jewellery. Rich women often had fancy hairstyles. A Roman writer wrote:

> She crimps her hair into rows of curls and builds it high, storey after storey.

Things to do

- Look at other parts of this book to find a picture of a Celt. What are the differences between Roman clothes and Celtic clothes?
- What differences can you think of between modern and Roman homes?

Roman food

In Roman homes, the main meal of the day was called 'cena'. It took place in the late afternoon. Rich people used expensive Samian bowls from Gaul. Friends were sometimes invited, but they had to bring their own cutlery and napkins! Jugglers, singers and poets were hired on special occasions.

This picture shows what a Roman kitchen may have looked like. The large jars were used for storing foods such as fish sauce, olive oil, wine or dried fruit. Some cooking was done in metal pots on a grill placed over a fire.
- Who do you think did the cooking and the washing-up?
- How were the houses heated and lit?

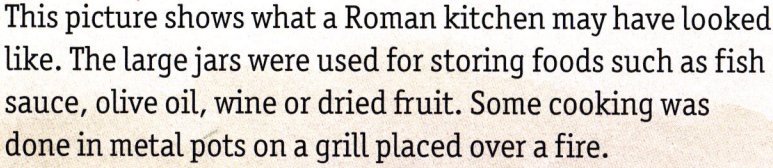

Shopping list for the forum: herbs, poppy seeds, honey, lettuce, wine, flour, nuts, pears, pheasant, dormice, suckling pig, snails, oysters, cheese, grapes

Things to find

- Look carefully around the kitchen and read the shopping list. What foods did the Romans like?
- Which do you think came from Britain and which had to be brought from other countries?
- Which of these do people in Britain still eat today?

X Leisure

Rich Romans had plenty of free time. They left many clues about what they did with their leisure.

What did the Romans do in their spare time?

A favourite meeting place of Romans was the public baths. Women and children usually bathed in the mornings and men in the afternoon and evening. Many people went to the baths every day.

This is a picture of the baths at Aquae Sulis, a Roman town which we now call Bath.
- Why do you think baths were popular with the Romans?
- What similar places do we have today?

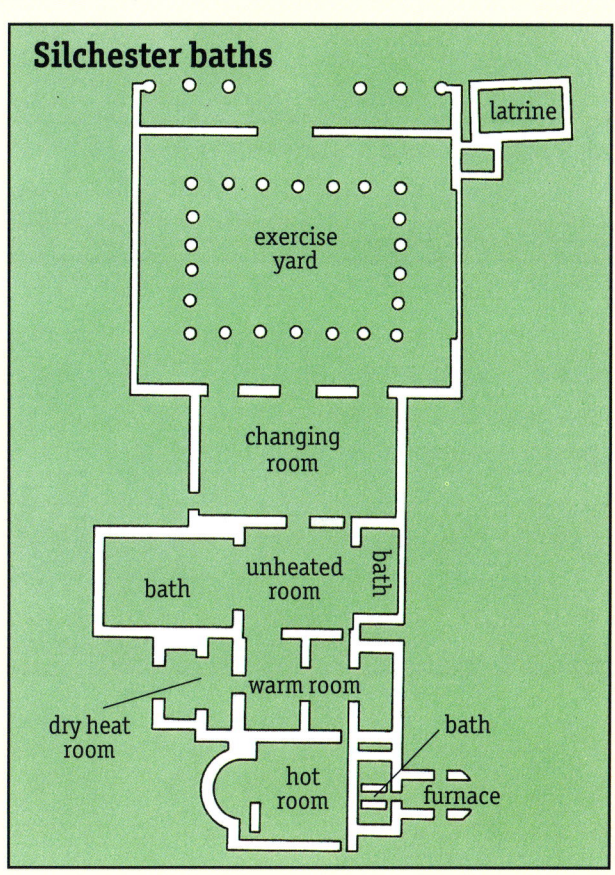

◀ This plan was made after the baths at Silchester were excavated.
- Look at the names of the rooms. Can you work out what they were each used for?

Many artefacts have been found at Silchester baths. Coins and animal bones have been found as well as the things in these photographs.

▲ board game

dice ▶

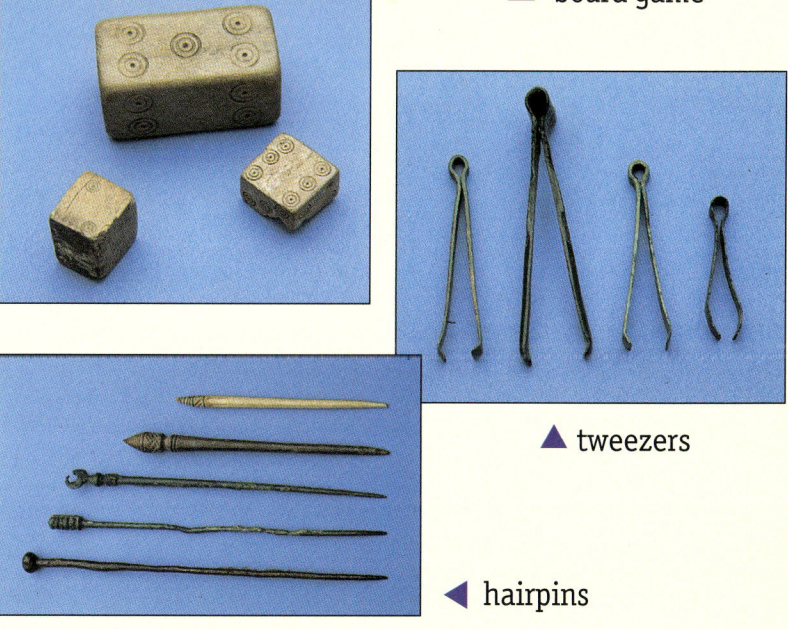

▲ tweezers

◀ hairpins

Think about

The Roman writer Tacitus said:

'Little by little the British began to enjoy the arcades, the bath houses and elegant dinner parties.'

- What does this tell you about how the British were beginning to live?

- Use these clues to work out what other things happened at the baths.

31

Roman entertainments

The Romans liked to go to theatres to see plays. The theatre at St Albans could hold about 5,000 people. It could have been used for religious celebrations as well as plays.

In some parts of the Roman Empire, like Italy and Greece, many big towns had their own theatre which people visited regularly. In Britain only five theatres have been discovered.

▲ This picture shows the remains of the Roman theatre in St Albans.
- Where was the stage?
- Were Roman theatres like theatres today? Explain your answer.
- Can you think of any reasons why there are so few Roman theatres in Britain?

32

The Romans also liked to see animal fights, wrestling matches, acrobatics and bear-baiting. They watched them in amphitheatres which had seats all around the central arena.

The most popular contests were the gladiator fights. Quite often gladiators were slaves who were made to fight. They were treated rather like pop stars are today. Their reward for winning contests was their freedom. Sometimes they could make a lot of money, too!

▲ This is what the Roman amphitheatre in Caerleon in Wales looks like today.

▲ This is called the Gladiator Vase.
  • How are the fighters' weapons and clothing different from those of the Roman soldiers on pages 8 and 9?

Things to do

- Find out some more about Roman amphitheatres, where they were usually found, and what they looked like. Draw a picture of what you find out.
- Write an argument between two children who cannot agree where to go. Each speech has been started for you.
  'I think we should go to the bath house because...'
  'No. I think we should go to the amphitheatre because...'

XI Religion

Because of the evidence archaeologists have found, we know that the Romans worshipped many gods. These gods were important in everyday life.

What did the Romans believe?

The Romans believed that spirits called 'lares' protected different parts of the home. They would have a statue of a lar in a little shrine in their house. The picture on the front of this book shows children making an offering in their shrine. Vesta protected the fire and the hearth. Janus, a god with two faces, looking both ways, was the god of the door. The 'penates' were the spirits who guarded the family store cupboard.

▲ This is a statue of the goddess Minerva. She is wearing a helmet and armour.
- Which Romans might have worshipped Minerva?

▶ This is a mosaic of the god Bacchus. He was the god of wine.
- What else could have been put in the picture to show who Bacchus was?

34

How did the Romans show their beliefs?

The Romans built special temples where they burned incense and prayed to their gods. They took gifts for the gods and hoped that, in return, the gods would take care of them. Archaeologists in Gloucestershire have found clues in a temple which helped them to work out which god was worshipped there. A statue of the god was found with hundreds of animal bones. Many chickens and sheep had been sacrificed to this god.

▲ This is a carving of the Roman messenger god, Mercury. He has a winged hat, a cloak over his left shoulder and carries a staff. At his feet are a chicken and a sheep.

▲ This modern picture shows what the Temple of Claudius probably looked like. The Roman people believed that their Emperor was a god. One of the first Roman temples in Britain was built for the Emperor Claudius in Colchester.

Think about

- Which god was being worshipped in the temple in Gloucestershire? (You will find a clue in the descriptions of gods on these pages.)

What did the Celts believe?

Like the Romans, the Celts were pagans and worshipped many gods. When the Romans invaded Britain they allowed the Celts to carry on worshipping their own gods. They even adopted some of the Celtic gods themselves. But the Romans did not like the Celtic priests, who were called Druids, because they were powerful leaders. Emperor Claudius banned the Druid religion.

▲ Archaeologists found this stone carving in the remains of a Roman temple. They think that it shows a Celtic god that the Romans chose to worship.
• What sort of god do you think this is?

▲ Here are three Celtic mother goddesses from Cirencester.
• How can you tell that they help with the harvest?

Christianity

When the Romans invaded Britain, a new religion called Christianity was spreading through the Roman Empire. Christians followed the teachings of Jesus Christ, who had lived in another part of the Roman Empire. The emperors thought the Christians were becoming too powerful and they killed many of them. Some of the soldiers who came to Britain were Christians.

About 250 years after the Romans came to Britain, Constantine became the emperor. He became a Christian and made Christianity the official religion of the Empire. Just as the early Christians had kept their beliefs secret, so some of the Celts carried on secretly believing in the old gods.

▲ A Christian symbol used the first two letters of Christ's name, written in Greek. This mosaic from a villa in Dorset uses this symbol behind the figure's head.
- Who could the figure in the picture be?

Things to do

- How do we know that:
  a sometimes the Romans let other people keep their own religions
  b sometimes the Romans tried to stop people having different beliefs?
- Compare the way the Romans showed their beliefs with the way people show their beliefs today.

XII Trade

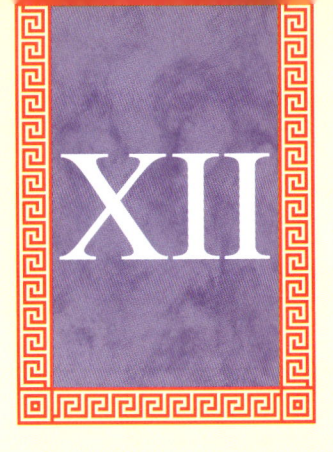

When the Romans came to Britain they wanted goods and food that they were used to. Things that could not be bought in Britain had to be brought from other countries by traders.

How did the Romans change trade?

The Celts did not have shops like ours. They made many things themselves from raw materials like gold, tin, lead, copper, iron and wool. They exchanged goods with other Celts. Exchanging goods without using money is called 'bartering'.

Most goods stayed in Britain, but by Caesar's time Celts were travelling to the Roman Empire to trade. They took woollen cloaks with hoods, rugs, beer, dogs and raw materials. These are called 'exports'. Goods that are brought into Britain from another country are called 'imports'.

▲ Soldiers could not barter. They were paid with coins like this. Celts began to take the coins in exchange for goods.

• Which export does this mosaic show?

The Romans drank a lot of wine and Britain could not make enough. They also needed glasses to drink from, but Britain made very little glass. So, glass and wine were imported.

- Look carefully at the chart showing trade in the Roman Empire and work out how wine and glasses got to Silchester.

Trade in the Roman Empire

← sea route to Britain

39

XIII Romanisation

Some Celts soon started to wear Roman clothes and live in Roman villas. They used Roman goods, food and coins, and spoke Latin. We say they became 'Romanised'. As time went on more Celtic families became Romanised. They were known as 'Roman-Britons'.

How 'Roman' did the Celts become?

Cogidumnus was the Celtic king of the Regni tribe. He made friends with the Roman leaders. He became a Roman citizen and changed his name to Tiberius Claudius Cogidumnus. He probably lived in a luxurious villa at Fishbourne, on the south coast of England.

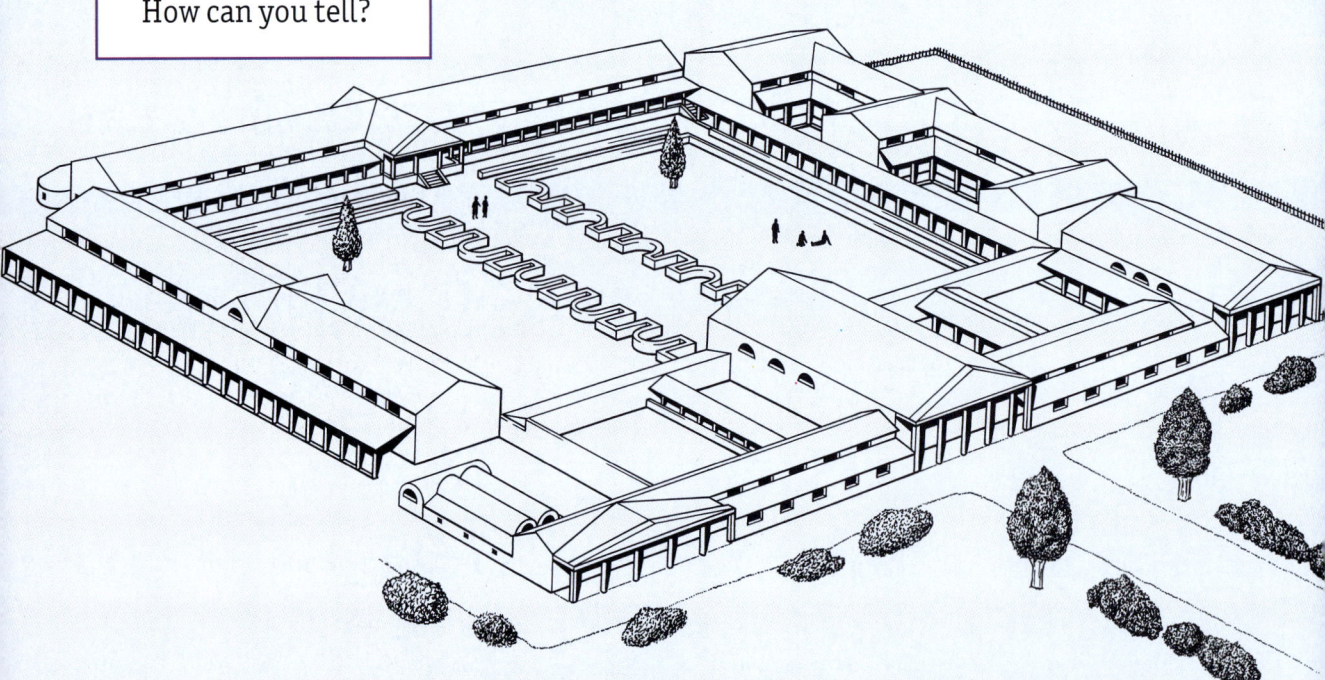

Think about

- Why was it a good idea for Cogidumnus to side with the Romans?
- Why did he change his name?
- Is his house Roman or Celtic in style? How can you tell?

▲ This is a line drawing of what archaeologists think the villa looked like when Cogidumnus lived there.

◀ This mosaic is from a villa in Yorkshire. It shows the goddess Venus.
- Compare this with the other mosaics in this book.
- Who do you think made the mosaic? What clues helped you to decide?

▼ This Samian Ware was imported from Gaul. It was very expensive to buy.
- What do you think it was used for?

▲ These pots were made by Celtic craftsmen who tried to copy Samian Ware.
- Why would they have done this?
- How well do you think they succeeded?

Things to do

- From each pair choose the person who was most likely to become Romanised. Would it be a person who:
  was rich or poor
  lived in the town or in the country
  lived in the south or in the north of Britain
  was a child or an adult?
- Look back at page 22. Which craftsman had become Romanised? How do you know?

XIV

The end of Roman Britain

About 300 years after the invasion of Britain, the Roman Empire started to break up. Gradually soldiers were taken away from Britain to fight in other countries. By AD 410 there was no Roman army left in Britain.

What happened to the Roman way of life?

Roman Britain was quite wealthy. People from other countries invaded Britain to take some of its wealth.

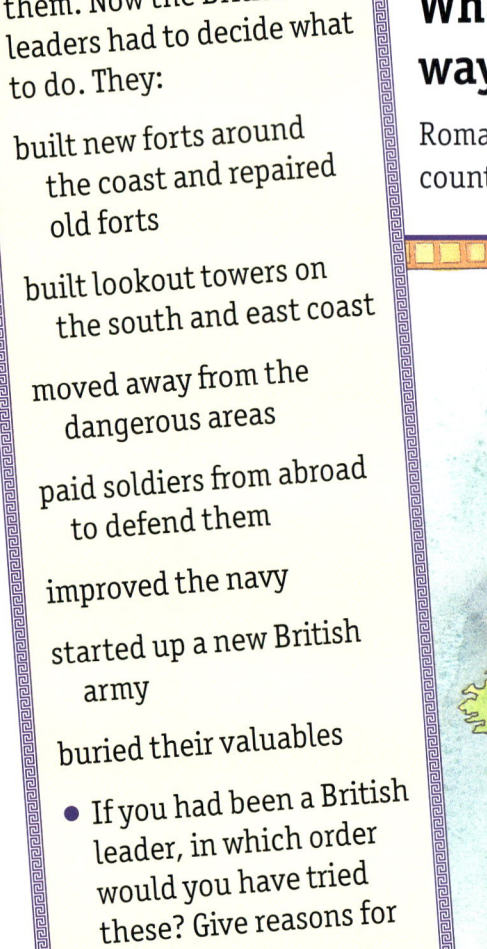

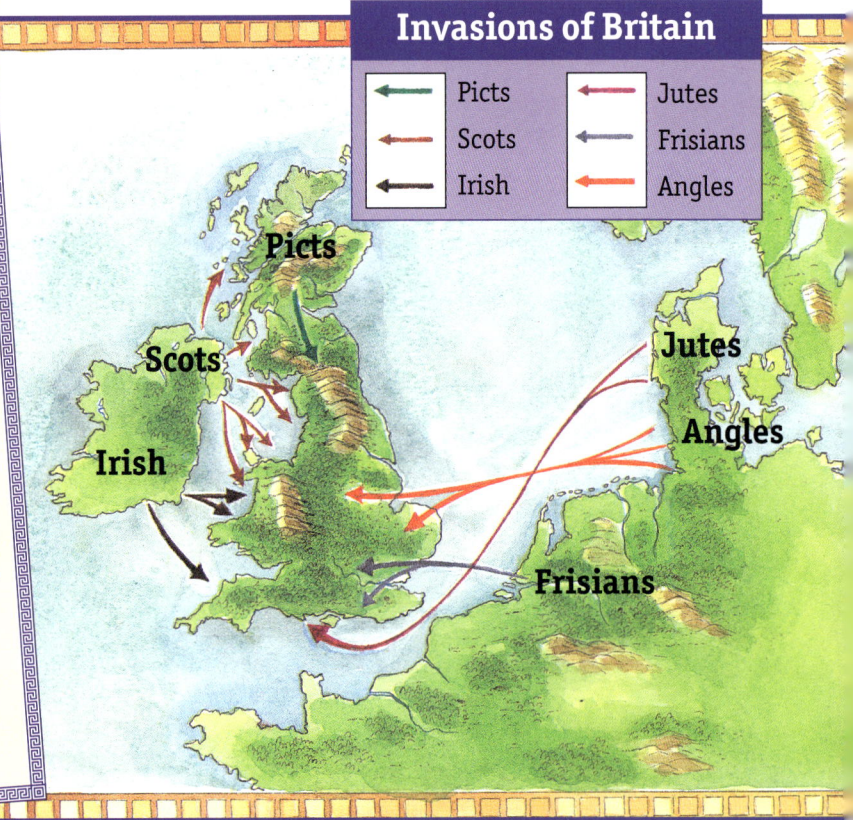

The Britons had relied on the Roman army to defend them. Now the British leaders had to decide what to do. They:

- built new forts around the coast and repaired old forts
- built lookout towers on the south and east coast
- moved away from the dangerous areas
- paid soldiers from abroad to defend them
- improved the navy
- started up a new British army
- buried their valuables

- If you had been a British leader, in which order would you have tried these? Give reasons for your answers.

Invasions of Britain

- Picts
- Scots
- Irish
- Jutes
- Frisians
- Angles

- Which peoples attacked Britain in the 4th and 5th centuries?

The Romans leave Britain

This is what happened when the Romans left Britain.
- Copy the chart, replacing the pictures with words.

No one organised repairs **SO** [picture of overgrown road]

[picture of attack on travellers] **SO** there was less trade.

People were frightened of attacks **SO** [picture of people building a fort]

[picture of ruined stone temple and wooden hut] **SO** people forgot how to build in stone.

New settlers came from Northern Europe **SO** [picture of Roman and Anglo-Saxon unable to understand each other: "I can't understand a word he's saying." / "Oft Scyld Scefing monegum mægthum meodosetla ofteah"]

[picture of days of the week and fallen statue of Mars] **SO** the old gods were forgotten.

People only grew enough food for themselves **SO** [picture of market with sign "NO CORN FOR BARTER"]

43

XV The Roman legacy

The remains of the Roman way of life are all around us. Here are some clues about what they left behind. Things in these pictures link us with the Romans who were here nearly 2,000 years ago.

How Roman are we today?

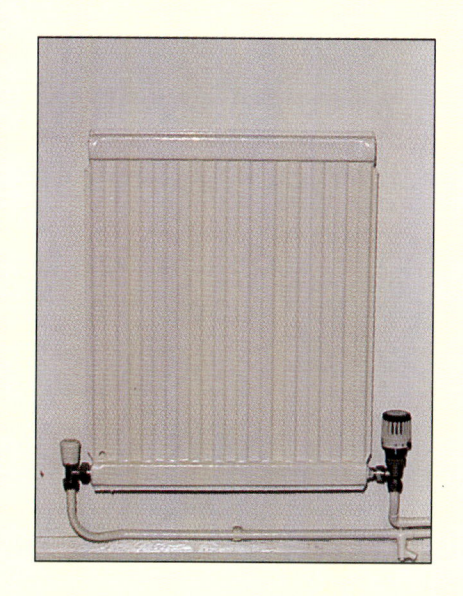

- Look at the pictures on these two pages. What part of the Roman legacy does each show?

45

How much did the Romans change Britain?

1 Many things changed when the Romans came to Britain. Look at the pictures on these pages. They show some of the things which changed. Think about each change in turn and answer these questions.
- Who did the change affect?
- Which parts of Britain changed?
- How quickly did it change?
- Did it change again when Roman rule ended?
- Can you think of any things which did not change at all?

2 Look back at page 2. Find the description of the different types of sources in this book. Find examples of each type of source in this book and in the work you have done.
- Which type of source did you find most useful? Why?
- There are some things about Roman Britain which the sources cannot tell us. How many can you think of?

3 Now that you have thought about the evidence, what is your answer to the question at the top of this page?

Roads

Language

Clothes

Houses

Food

Religion

47

Index

A amphitheatres 19, 33
archaeologists 2, 18, 19, 20, 22, 26, 35, 36, 40
army 5, 14, 15
artefacts 2, 7, 22, 23, 31

B baths 19, 21, 25, 30, 31, 45
Boudica 3, 16, 17

C Celts 2, 3, 6, 7, 10, 14, 16, 20, 24, 25, 36, 38, 40, 41
Christianity 37
Claudius 3, 4, 5, 10, 16, 35, 36
clothes, Celtic 6, 7, 10, 16, 17, 46
clothes, Roman 23, 27, 38, 40, 47
Colchester 10, 14, 16, 35

D Druids 16, 36

F farming 3, 6, 7, 24, 25, 36
food 24, 28, 29, 40, 45, 47
forts (Roman) 12, 13, 15, 18, 42
forum 18, 19, 29

G gladiators 33
gods, Celtic 36, 37
gods, Roman 13, 16, 34, 35, 36, 43, 47

H Hadrian's Wall 3, 12, 13, 18
hill-forts 7, 10, 11
houses, Roman 20, 21, 25, 26, 29, 47
hypocaust 21, 25

I Iceni 3, 16
invasions 3, 4, 5, 42

J jewellery, Celtic 7, 17
jewellery, Roman 23, 27
Julius Caesar 2, 4, 38

L Latin 16, 22, 40, 46
London 14, 16

M mosaics 20, 25, 26, 34, 37, 38, 41

P pottery 22, 28, 33, 41

R raw materials 5, 6, 7, 23, 24, 26, 38
religion 9, 13, 32, 34, 35, 36, 43, 44, 47
roads 14, 15, 18, 19, 25, 43, 44, 46
Roman Empire 2, 4, 5, 32, 37, 39, 42

S shops 18, 20, 38
Silchester 14, 18, 19, 20, 22, 23, 31, 39
slaves 6, 14, 16, 25, 33
soldiers 8, 9, 10, 13, 14, 16, 18, 37, 38, 42

T temples 13, 16, 19, 35, 36
theatres 32, 44
tools 22
towns 18, 19, 20, 21, 22, 26, 45
trade 3, 13, 38, 43
tribes 2, 3, 10, 16, 18, 40

V villas 25, 37, 40, 41

W weapons 8, 9, 10. 11